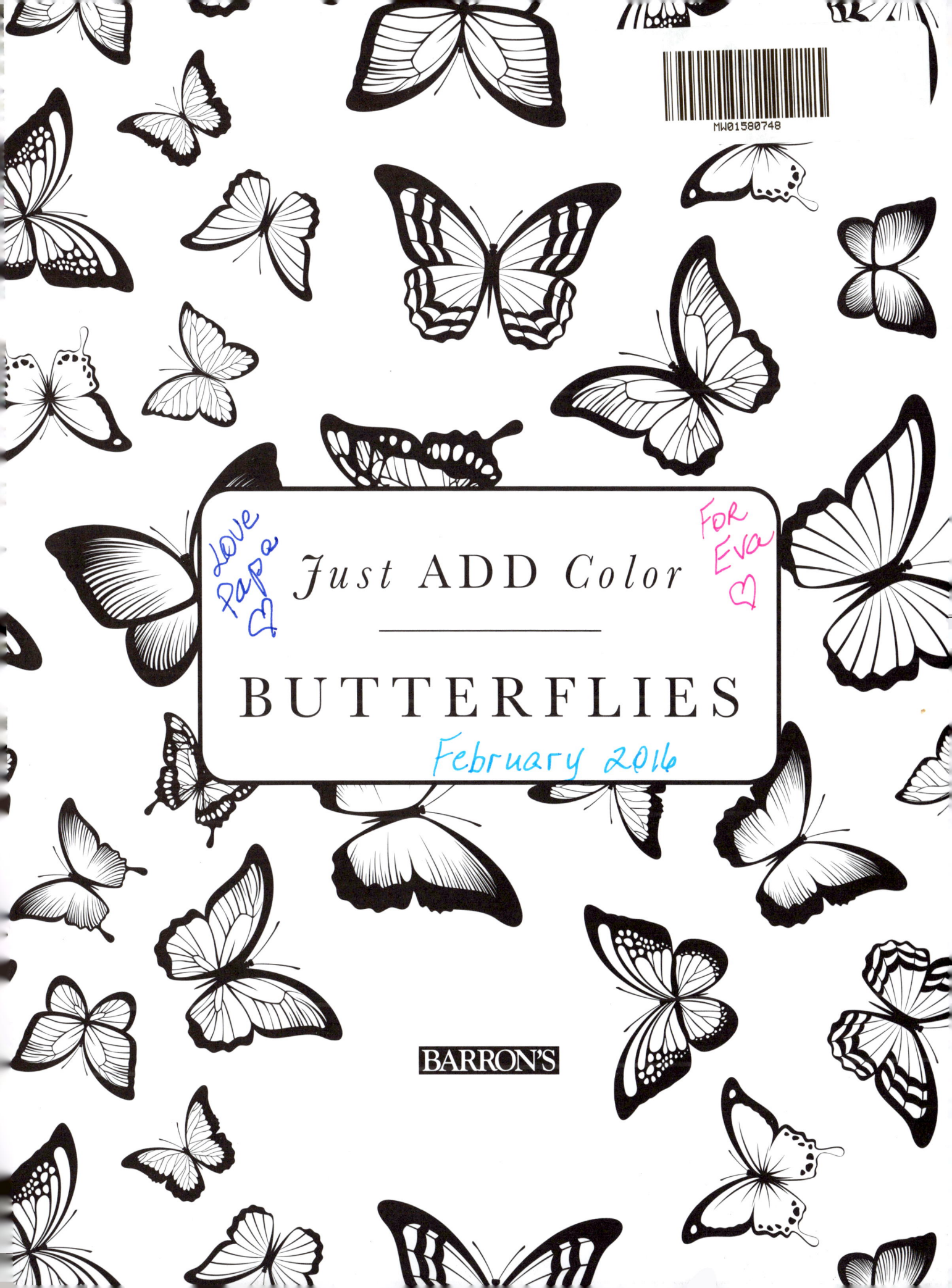

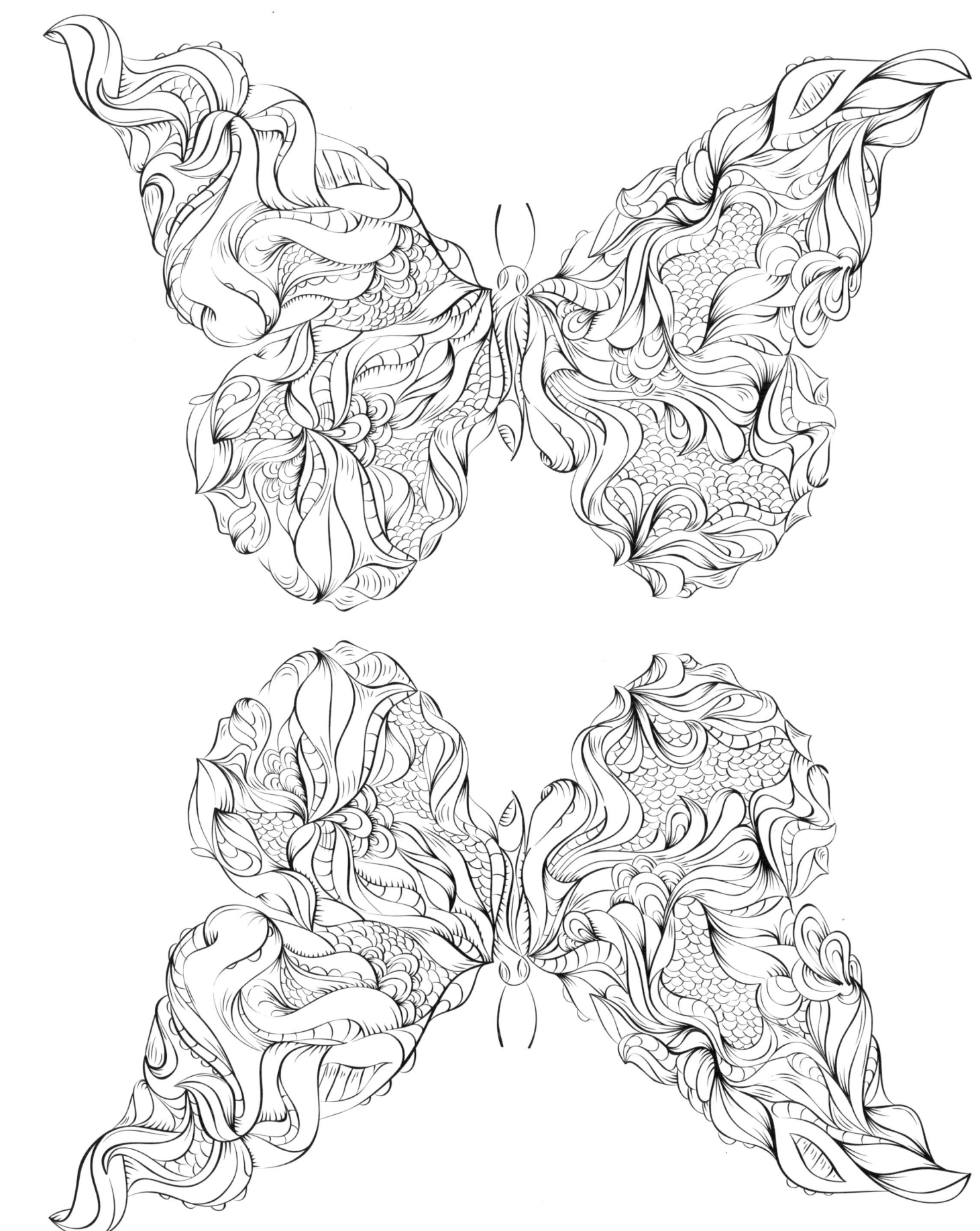

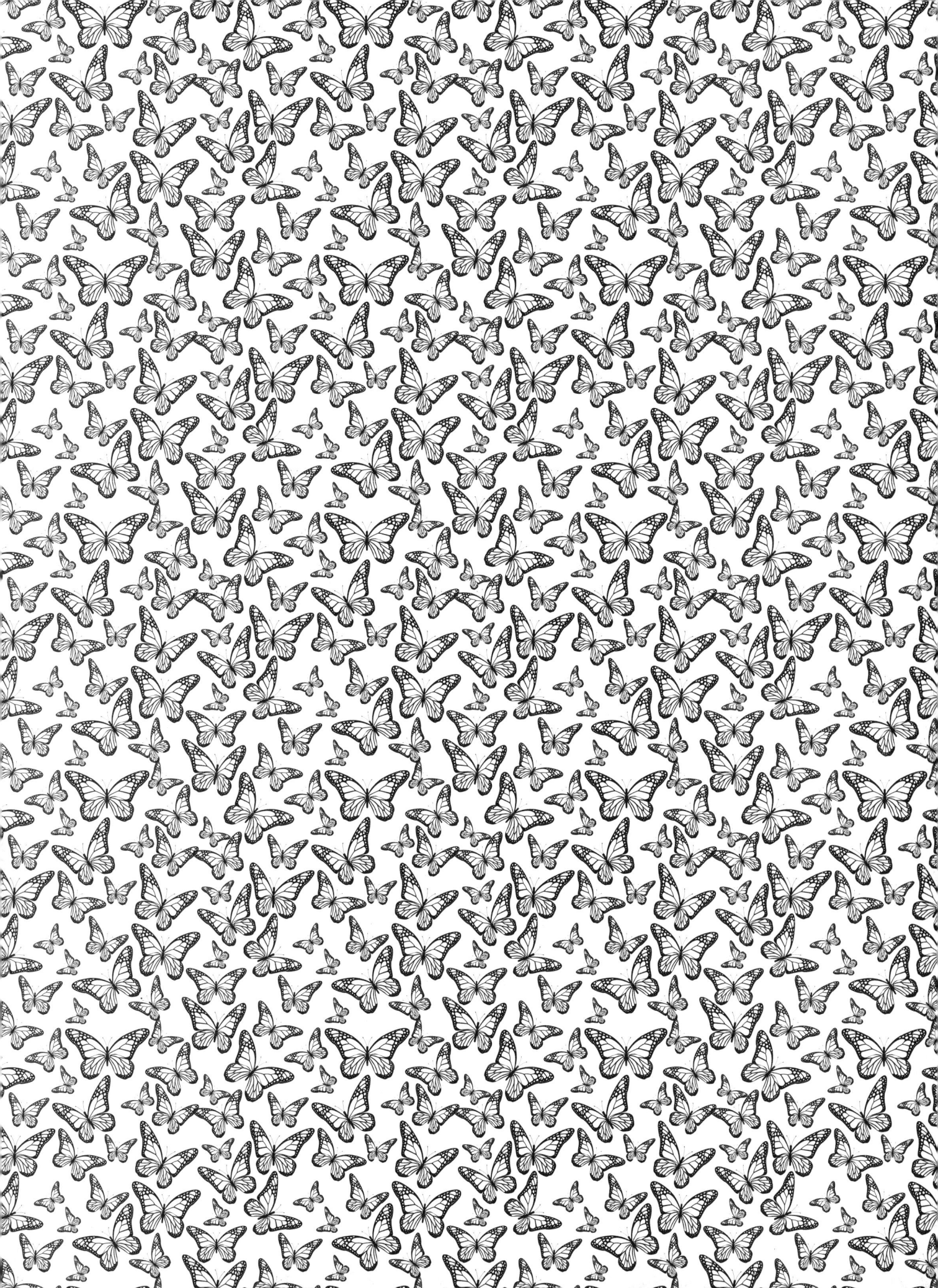

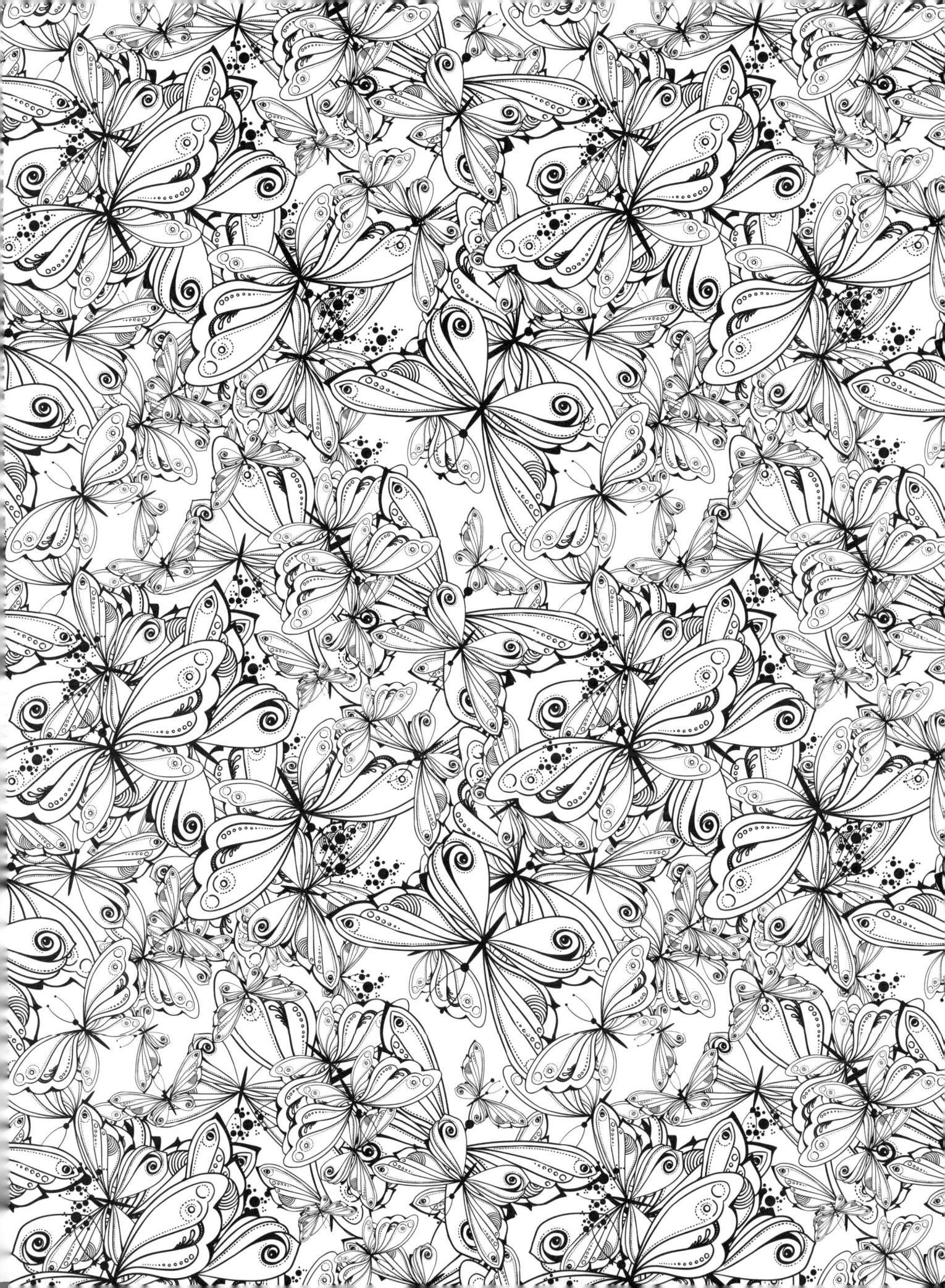

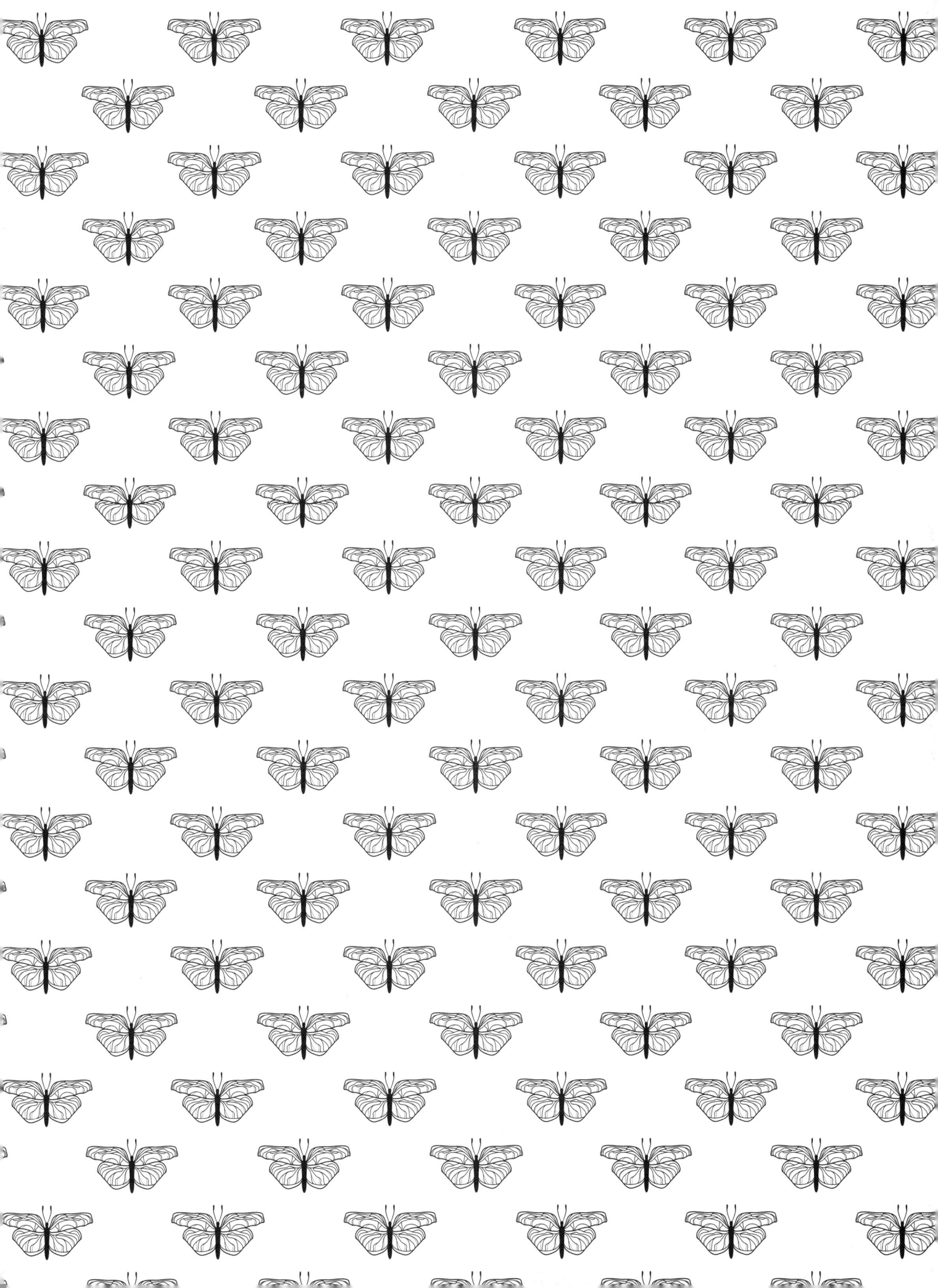

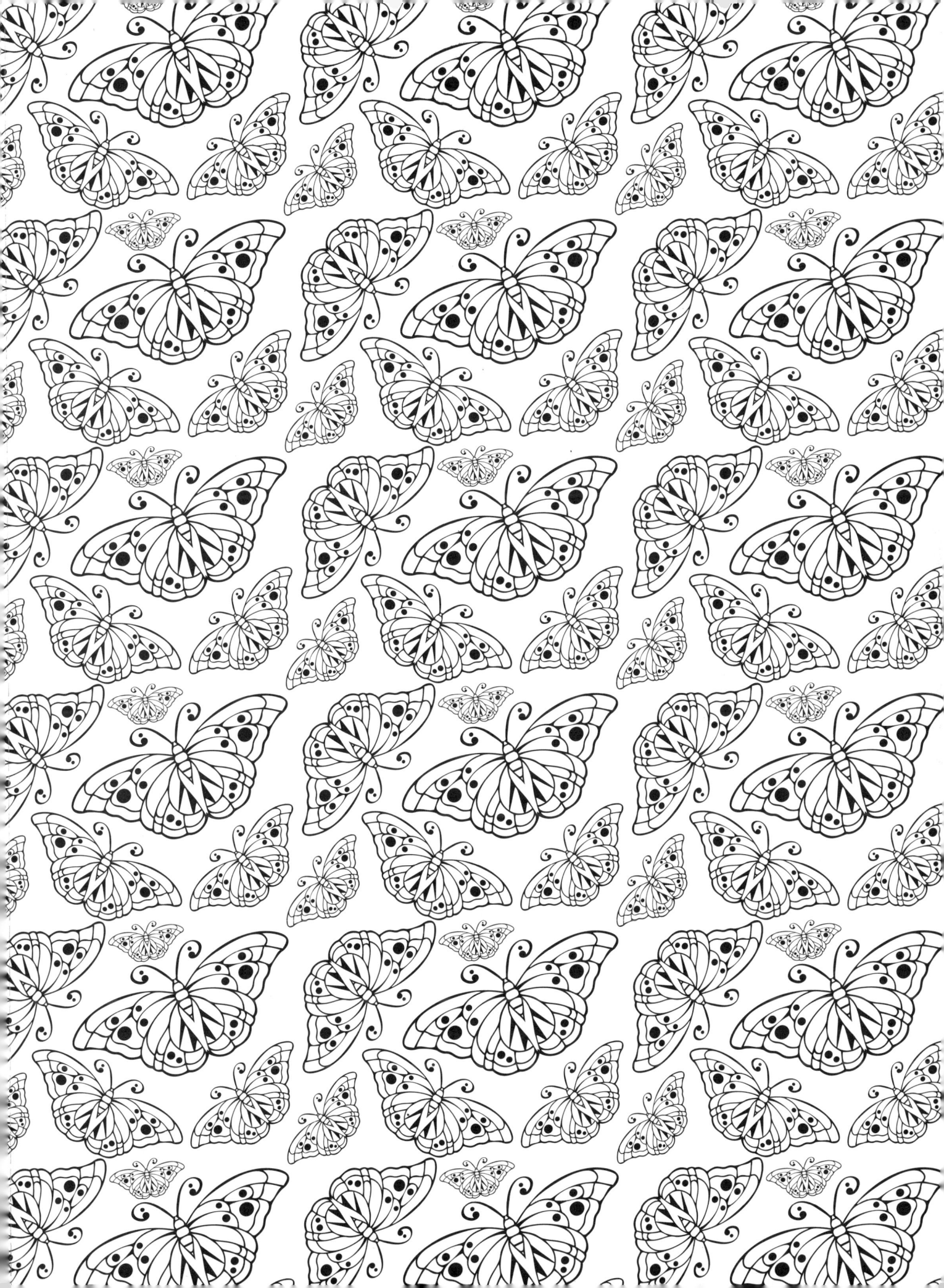

First edition for North America published in 2016 by Barron's Educational Series, Inc.

© Copyright 2016 by Carlton Publishing Group

All rights reserved.

No part of this publication may be reproduced or distributed in any form or by any means without the written permission of the copyright owner.

All inquiries should be addressed to:

Barron's Educational Series, Inc.
250 Wireless Boulevard
Hauppauge, New York 11788
www.barronseduc.com

ISBN: 978-1-4380-0806-6

Manufactured by Marquis, Louiseville, Canada

Printed in Canada

9 8 7 6 5 4 3 2

For best results, colored pencils are recommended.